I Am With You Always

Inspirational books by Douglas Bloch

Words That Heal
Listening To Your Inner Voice
I Am With You Always

I AM
WITH YOU
ALWAYS

*A Treasury of Inspirational
Quotations, Poems, and Prayers*

Douglas Bloch

BANTAM BOOKS
NEW YORK · TORONTO
LONDON · SYDNEY · AUCKLAND

I AM WITH YOU ALWAYS
A Bantam Book / September 1992

See page 208 for acknowledgments

Library of Congress Cataloging-in-Publication Data
Bloch, Douglas, 1949–
    I am with you always : a treasury of inspirational quotations,
poems, and prayers / Douglas Bloch.
        p.   cm.
    ISBN 0–553–35404–3
    1. Religion—Quotations, maxims, etc.   2. Religious poetry.
3. Prayers.   I. Title.
PN6084.R3B56   1992
082—dc20   92–3193
                                                         CIP

Published simultaneously in the United States and Canada

Bantam Books are published by Bantam Books, a division of Bantam Doubleday
Dell Publishing Group, Inc. Its trademark, consisting of the words "Bantam
Books" and the portrayal of a rooster, is Registered in U.S. Patent and Trademark
Office and in other countries. Marca Registrada. Bantam Books, 1540 Broadway,
New York, New York 10036.

PRINTED IN THE UNITED STATES OF AMERICA

CWO   0 9 8 7 6 5 4 3 2

To the spirit of truth that dwells in each of us

Lo, I am with you always,
even unto the end of the world.

Matthew 28:20

❦

The purpose of this book is to provide you with a broad sampling of inspirational quotations, poems, and prayers from the world's great spiritual teachings and literature. These words were chosen to serve as gentle reminders of your connection to the spirit of truth and to help you communicate with your own inner teacher. The text is organized around specific themes so that you can easily locate the appropriate quotation to speak to your particular needs.

The presence of God is always with us, although we may let fear and doubt convince us that it is separate and removed. *I Am With You Always* is designed to support our connection with that Source—in which we live, move, and have our being. In the midst of our joy and sorrow, gain and loss, hope and despair, a loving energy gently guides us. We need only affirm and give thanks for the gift that is already given.

We are like the man who dreamed he saw two sets of footprints while walking along the beach, one his own and one belonging to God. During a difficult time, however, he dreamed he saw only one set. Thinking God had abandoned him, the man cried out and asked why he was now alone. The Infinite replied, "I would never leave you. When you saw only one set of footprints, it was then that I carried you."

Douglas Bloch
September 17, 1991
Portland, Oregon

CONTENTS

I AM WITH YOU ALWAYS . . .

. . . to help you provide for your every need.

. . . to guide and direct your way.

❧

I AM WITH YOU ALWAYS . . .

. . . to heal your relationships with others.

. . . to help you move through the pain.

I AM WITH YOU ALWAYS . . .

. . . to lead you into the fullness of joy.

We Create Through Our Thoughts

We are creative beings, and the tool by which we create is THOUGHT. A proverb states, "Thoughts held in the mind produce after their kind." If you wish to change the outer circumstances of your life, you can begin by focusing on your inner world.

Everything in the physical world started out as an idea. The chair in which you are sitting, the objects in the room—all these first took form in someone's mind. The universe itself may have begun as an idea in the mind of God.

There is tremendous power in focusing on positive and uplifting thoughts. Like attracts like. When you expect the best, you create a thought field that draws to you the desired result. Let your thoughts be kind, truthful, and supportive and so will be the world in which you live.

The greatest revolution in our generation
is the discovery that human beings,
by changing the inner attitudes of their minds,
can change the outer aspects of their lives.
William James

As he thinketh in his heart, so is he.
Proverbs 23:7

There is nothing more potent than thought.
Deed follows word and word follows thought.
The word is the result of a mighty thought,
and where the thought is mighty and pure
the result is always mighty and pure.
Gandhi

Mind is the master power that molds and makes,
And we are mind, and evermore we take,
The tool of thought and shaping what we will,
Bring forth a thousand joys, a thousand ills.
We think in secret and it comes to pass—
Environment is but our looking glass.
James Allen

The mind is its own place, and in itself
Can make a heav'n of hell, a hell of heav'n.
John Milton

There is nothing either good or bad,
but thinking makes it so.
Shakespeare

He gave man speech, and speech created thought,
Which is the measure of the universe.
Percy Bysshe Shelley

Thou shalt also decree a thing,
and it shall be established unto thee.
Job 22:28

All that we are is the result of what we have thought.
Buddha

Whatsoever things are true,
whatsoever things are honest,
whatsoever things are just,
whatsoever things are pure,
whatsoever things are lovely,
whatsoever things are of good report;
if there be any virtue, and if there be any praise,
think on these things.
Philippians 4:8

Great thoughts always come from the heart.
French Proverb

Great men are they who see that spiritual is stronger than any material force, that thoughts rule the world.
Ralph Waldo Emerson

Our life is what our thoughts make it.
Marcus Aurelius

They can do all because they think they can.
Virgil

The Power of Choice

One of the most important aspects of our humanhood is having the power to choose. Our loving Creator has allowed us to choose the world in which we will live. If we choose to be loving in thought, word, and deed, we create a loving world. If we choose thoughts or actions of fear or ill will, then these qualities will fill the world we inhabit.

Having free will means being able to choose anew. Nothing is permanently fixed. Through making new choices, the past can be healed and pain and suffering can be released from our lives.

Even when we cannot choose our outer conditions, we can still choose how we will respond to them. This is the ultimate *freedom.* By choosing to see every situation as contributing to our highest good, we can transform even the most difficult circumstances into blessings.

It lies within ourselves or our own actions
to possess happiness;
or by sloth and negligence
to fall from happiness into ruin.
Origen

It matters not how strait the gate,
How charged with punishments the scroll,
I am the master of my fate:
I am the captain of my soul.
William Ernest Henley

You create your reality according to your beliefs.
Yours is the creative energy that makes your world.
Jane Roberts

Whatever you vividly imagine,
ardently desire,
sincerely believe,
and enthusiastically act upon
must inevitably come to pass.
Paul Meyer

Life is what our character makes it.
We fashion it as a snail does his shell.
Jules Renard

Be there a will, and wisdom finds a way.
George Crabbe

Every moment of your life is infinitely creative,
and the universe is endlessly bountiful.
Just put forward a clear enough request,
and everything your heart desires must come to you.
Shakti Gawain

People are always blaming their circumstances
for what they are.
I don't believe in circumstances.
The people who get on in this world
are the people who get up
and look for the circumstances they want,
and if they can't find them, make them.
George Bernard Shaw

Destiny is not a matter of chance,
it is a matter of choice.
William Jennings Bryan

A true lover of God can inspire his brothers and sisters
with a desire to return to their home in Him;
but they themselves, step by step,
must make the actual journey.
Paramahansa Yogananda

Don't feel sorry for yourself if you have taken the
wrong road—turn around!
Anonymous

To reach the port of Heaven,
we must sail sometimes with the wind,
sometimes against it,
but we must sail, and not drift, nor lie at anchor.
Oliver Wendell Holmes

Follow Your Dream

As human beings, we are born dreamers. It is natural to build our lives around a vision or purpose that gives meaning to our existence. Pursuing your heart's desire transforms life into a wondrous journey. Each day becomes an exciting adventure. Even your defeats are seen as learning experiences that bring you one step closer to the cherished goal.

Following your dream invokes spiritual aid from unexpected sources. All manner of assistance comes to you that otherwise would not have appeared. Opportunities arise that moments before did not exist; doors open that were previously closed; invisible hands reach out to guide and direct your way.

As you align yourself with your higher purpose, the universe cannot help but make straight, smooth, and perfect your way. Even when challenges arise, you still retain the joy that your vision brings. As impractical as it may seem, the safest, most dependable, and most secure way to lead your life is to follow your dream.

There is only one success—
to be able to spend your life in your own way.
Christopher Morley

For where your treasure is,
there will your heart be also.
Matthew 6:21

Do not follow where the path may lead.
Go instead where there is no path, and leave a trail.
Anonymous

You see things; and you say, "Why?"
But I dream things that never were; and I say,
"Why not?"
George Bernard Shaw

If you have built castles in the air,
your work need not be lost;
that is where they should be.
Now put the foundations under them.
Henry David Thoreau

Ah, but a man's reach should exceed his grasp,
Or what's a heaven for?
Robert Browning

Hold fast to dreams for if dreams die,
Life is a broken-winged bird that cannot fly.
Hold fast to dreams for when dreams go,
Life is a barren field frozen with snow.
Langston Hughes

You are never given a wish without also being given the
power to make it true.
You may have to work for it, however.
Richard Bach

Whatever you can do, or dream you can, begin it;
Boldness has genius, power and magic in it.
Begin it now.
Goethe

The great thing in this world
is not so much where we stand,
but in what direction we are moving.
Oliver Wendell Holmes

I dream, therefore I am.
Anonymous

Follow your bliss.
Joseph Campbell

When you are inspired by a dream,
God has hit the ball into your court.
Now you have to hit it back with commitment.
Robert Schuller

If one advances confidently
in the direction of his dreams,
and endeavors to live the life which he has imagined,
he will meet with a success unexpected
in common hours.
Henry David Thoreau

❣

Know Thyself

"Know thyself." This motto of the ancient Greeks is as important today as it was thousands of years ago. A person who knows himself—mentally, emotionally, and spiritually—is the master of himself and his life. There is no obstacle in the world that he cannot overcome.

As a species, we have mastered the external world, but we are still a mystery to ourselves. We explore the farthest reaches of outer space, but the inner space of the psyche remains uncharted. Because of this lack of self-knowledge, we have created havoc for ourselves and the planet.

It is time that humanity attain a new level of spiritual maturity and move from adolescence to adulthood. It is time to let go of selfishness and greed and live the central teaching of the world's religions— love thy neighbor as thyself. Only a knowledge and experience of our spiritual natures will create a shift in consciousness so that the long-awaited transformation may at last take place.

He that ruleth his spirit is greater than he
that taketh a city.
Proverbs 16:32

He who goes to the bottom of his own heart
knows his own nature;
and knowing his own nature, he knows heaven.
Mencius of China

He who knows others is wise;
He who knows himself is enlightened.
Lao-tzu

Know then thyself, presume not God to scan;
The proper study of mankind is man.
Alexander Pope

Our remedies oft in ourselves do lie.
Shakespeare

There is only one corner of the universe
you can be certain of improving,
and that's your own self.
Aldous Huxley

Know thyself.
Be thyself.
Master thyself.
Anonymous

Wisdom is the principal thing;
therefore get wisdom:
and with all thy getting get understanding.
Proverbs 4:7

What lies behind us
and what lies before us
are tiny matters
compared to what lies within us.
Ralph Waldo Emerson

*But what is a man profited, if he shall gain the whole
world, and lose his own soul?
or what shall a man give in exchange for his soul?*
Matthew 16:26

The life which is unexamined is not worth living.
Socrates

*Those who cannot remember the past
are condemned to repeat it.*
George Santayana

Oh wad some power the giftie gie us,
To see oursels as others see us!
Robert Burns

Search thine own heart. What paineth thee
In others in thyself may be.
John Greenleaf Whittier

Go to your bosom;
Knock there, and ask your heart what it doth know.
Shakespeare

It is far more important that one's life
should be perceived
than that it should be transformed;
for no sooner has it been perceived,
than it transforms itself of its own accord.
Maurice Maeterlinck

Wherever we go, whatever we do,
self is the sole subject we study and learn.
Ralph Waldo Emerson

When we cannot find contentment in ourselves
it is useless to seek it elsewhere.
La Rochefoucauld

Although all men have a common destiny,
each individual must also work out
his personal salvation for himself. . . .
In the last analysis, each is responsible
for "finding himself."
Thomas Merton

There is no one without faults, even men of God.
They are men of God not because they are faultless,
but because they know their own faults,
do not hide them,
and are ever ready to correct themselves.
Gandhi

Turn It Over

There comes a time in any undertaking when we have done all that we can do. Having accomplished what is humanly possible, it is time to turn the rest over to God.

Turning it over is akin to planting a seed in the ground and having the faith to allow that seed to germinate in darkness. Just as invisible forces bring forth the seed's potential, Infinite Intelligence works behind the scenes to produce the good that you desire. As one person put it, "I realize that God is doing for me what I cannot do for myself."

Turning it over also means placing the final results in God's hands. Have faith that if spirit is doing the work through you, spirit will handle the outcome. As you develop this trust in the higher plan, fear and worry will gradually disappear until you can declare with confidence, "It is all for Your glory. It is all in Your hands, and I do rejoice in this."

Come unto me, all ye that labour and are heavy laden,
and I will give you rest. . . .
For my yoke is easy, and my burden is light.
Matthew 11:28–30

Cast thy burden upon the Lord,
and he shall sustain thee.
Psalm 55:22

I am the ocean and can absorb all your burden.
Meher Baba

As children bring their broken toys
with tears for us to mend,
I brought my broken dreams to God,
because He was my friend.
But then, instead of leaving Him in peace
to work alone,
I hung around and tried to help,
with ways that were my own.
At last I snatched them back and cried,
"How could you be so slow?"
"My child," He said, "what could I do?
You never did let go."
Anonymous

The universe handles the details.
Arnold Patent

We set the sail; God makes the wind.
Anonymous

Let go and let God.
Alcoholics Anonymous

Sow the seeds of truth, but do not continue to scratch them up—leave the results to Him.
Edgar Cayce

Answered Prayers

We live in a responsive universe. The spiritual law of demand and supply says that supply comes in response to a demand or request we make. When we ask with a sincere and open heart, the universe *must* answer. Infinite Intelligence, God, is ever ready to fulfill our smallest or greatest requests.

Sometimes the answer may be other than we are expecting or something we don't want to hear. Let the Infinite decide how your supply should come, for it knows best what is for your highest good.

Besides asking for the good you seek, you will need to take concrete steps to make it happen. Pray as if everything depended on God, but act as if everything depended on you.

Finally, let your request be for the benefit of yourself *and* others. You will not be denied if what you are seeking is for the highest good of all concerned.

We walk and talk with the Father within.
We have but to speak and He answers.
Ernest Holmes

Ask, and it shall be given you; seek, and ye shall find;
knock, and it shall be opened unto you:
For every one that asketh receiveth;
and he that seeketh findeth;
and to him that knocketh, it shall be opened.
Matthew 7:7–8

All prayers are answered when the individual doesn't tell
God just how to answer them.
Anonymous

Be careful for nothing; but in every thing
by prayer and supplication with thanksgiving
let your requests be made known to God.
Phillipians 4:6

All things, whatever ye shall ask in prayer, believing,
ye shall receive.
Matthew 21:22

So long as people in this world are crying for help,
I shall return to ply my boat
and offer to take them to the heavenly shores.
Paramahansa Yogananda

And it shall come to pass,
that before they call, I will answer;
and while they are yet speaking, I will hear.
Isaiah 65:24

Be careful what you ask for; for it may come to pass.
Native American Saying

We Reap What We Sow

We are all enrolled in a school called "life on earth." The way we learn in this school is through cause and effect. Also known as the law of karma, it states that whatever we sow in thought, word, or deed is that which we reap.

The principle of cause and effect shows us that we are responsible for our lives. It says that we can create whatever we want if we are willing to take the necessary steps. Without this principle, we would be unable to learn from experience, for we would see no relationship between our actions and the consequences of those actions.

A loving universe shows us how what we express and what we experience are connected. If we sow love, we reap love; if we sow hate, then that is what we reap. Through experiencing both the pleasant and painful results of our actions, we slowly learn to choose the good. This is the blessing of reaping what we sow.

Be not deceived; God is not mocked:
for whatsoever a man soweth, that shall he also reap.
Galatians 6:7

For know that each soul constantly meets its own self.
No problem may be run away from. Meet it now.
Edgar Cayce

Who has not reaped what he hath sown?
Wheat springs from wheat and barley from barley.
Sikh Proverb

Act maketh joy and woe.
What hath been bringeth what shall be.
Buddha

I will render to the man according to his work.
Proverbs 24:29

The tissue of the Life to be
We weave with colors all our own,
And in the field of Destiny
We reap as we have sown.
John Greenleaf Whittier

Thou canst not gather what thou didst not sow;
As thou dost plant a tree, so will it grow.
The Laws of Manu

Ye shall know them by their fruits.
Do men gather grapes of thorns,
or figs of thistles?
Matthew 7:16

Nothing can be created from nothing.
Lucretius

The sower may mistakenly sow his peas crookedly;
The peas make no mistake,
but come up and show his line.
Ralph Waldo Emerson

In nature, there are neither punishments nor rewards—
there are consequences.
Chinese Proverb

Glorious is the fruit of good labors.
Solomon

❦

I Am With You Always

It is impossible for you to be separated from your
spiritual nature. No matter how alone you may feel, you
are never truly alone, for you live, move, and have your
being in spiritual consciousness. This presence can never
leave or forsake you. As Jesus told his disciples, "Lo, I
am with you always, even unto the end of the world."

Nevertheless, there are times when we feel cut
off from our source. But God has not gone anywhere.
Through our doubts and fears, we have temporarily
blocked our experience of the Divine. As they say in
Alcoholics Anonymous, "If God seems far away, who
moved?"

We can reopen the channels by learning to
listen for that "still small voice" within. Each day, we
can go into the silence and connect with the indwelling
presence. If we faithfully establish and deepen this
connection, we will know and feel the truth of the
Spirit's wonderful promise, "I am with you always."

❦

Whither shall I go from thy spirit?
or whither shall I flee from thy presence?
If I ascend up into heaven, thou art there:
if I make my bed in hell, behold, thou art there.
If I take the wings of the morning, and
dwell in the uttermost parts of the sea;
Even there shall thy hand lead me,
and thy right hand shall hold me.
Psalm 139:7–10

God is not far from the seeker,
nor is it impossible to see Him.
He is like the sun which is ever shining right above you.
Meher Baba

❦

Do you need Me? I am there.
You cannot see Me, yet I am the light you see by.
You cannot hear Me, yet I speak through your voice.
You cannot feel Me,
yet I am the power at work in your hands.
I am at work, though you do not understand My ways.
I am at work, though you do not recognize My works.
I am not strange visions. I am not mysteries.
Only in absolute stillness, beyond self,
can you know Me as I am,
and then but as a feeling and a faith.
Yet I am there. Yet I am here. Yet I answer.
When you need Me, I am there.
Even if you deny Me, I am there.
Even when you feel most alone, I am there.
Even in your fears, I am there.
Even in your pain, I am there.
I am there when you pray and when you do not pray.
Though your faith in Me is unsure,
My faith in you never wavers,
because I know you, because I love you.
Beloved, I am there.
James Dillet Freeman

The Lord . . . be not far from every one of us;
For in him we live, and move, and have our being.
Acts 17:27–28

God resides in every human form and
in every particle of his creation.
Gandhi

Self-realization is the knowing—
in body mind and soul—
that we are one with the omnipresence of God.
Paramahansa Yogananda

I take for my sureties:
The power of God to guide me,
The might of God to uphold me,
The wisdom of God to teach me,
The eye of God to watch over me,
The ear of God to hear me,
The word of God to give me speech,
The hand of God to protect me,
The way of God to go before me,
The shield of God to shelter me. . . .
Christ be with me, Christ before me,
Christ behind me, Christ within me,
Christ beneath me, Christ above me,
Christ at my right, Christ at my left,
Christ in the heart of every man who thinks of me,
Christ in the mouth of every man who speaks to me,
Christ in every eye that sees me,
Christ in every ear that hears me.
Prayer of St. Patrick

He who perceives Me everywhere,
and beholds everything in Me,
never loses sight of Me nor do I ever lose sight of him.
Krishna

The task ahead of us is never as great
as the Power behind us.
Alcoholics Anonymous

Put God First

There is only one basic desire that motivates the spiritual seeker—to make the experience of God, of divine bliss and joy, the center of the life experience.

We are spiritual beings living in a material universe, and as such, our first priority is to nurture that eternal part of us. The eleventh step of AA's twelve-step program states it beautifully: "Sought through prayer and meditation to improve our conscious contact with God *as we understood Him,* praying only for knowledge of His will for us and the power to carry that out."

When we become one with our higher self and let it govern our life, "all things" are added unto us. From this state of elevated awareness, everything falls into place. Worry and anxiety diminish as divine love guides and directs our steps. There is no deeper peace than this.

Thou shalt love the Lord thy God with all thy heart,
and with all thy soul, and with all thy mind.
Matthew 22:37

Love of God is the essence of all spiritual discipline.
Ramakrishna

You made us after yourself O Lord,
and we cannot find repose except in thee.
St. Augustine

God alone is Real, and the goal of life
is to become united with Him through Love.
Meher Baba

The glory of God is great.
He is real and He can be found.
Silently and surely as you walk on the path of life,
you must come to the realization
that God is the only object, the only goal
that will satisfy you; for in God
lies the answer to every desire of the human heart.
Paramahansa Yogananda

Silence thy thoughts and fix thy whole attention
on thy Master,
whom thou dost not see, but whom thou feelest.
Madame Blavatsky

Everywhere, wherever you may find yourself,
you can set up an altar to God
in your mind by means of prayer.
Way of a Pilgrim

The worship of God is not a rule of safety—
it is an adventure of the spirit.
Alfred North Whitehead

Reflect that someday you will suddenly have to leave
everything in this world,
so make the acquaintance of God now.
Lahiri Mahasaya

And ye shall seek me, and find me
when ye shall search for me with all your heart.
Jeremiah 29:13

The best form in which to worship God is every form.
Neem Karoli Baba

Therefore take no thought, saying,
What shall we eat? or, What shall we drink? or,
Wherewithal shall we be clothed?
. . . for your heavenly Father
knoweth that ye have need of all these things.
But seek ye first the kingdom of God,
and his righteousness;
and all these things shall be added unto you.
Matthew 6:31–33

The Presence Within

Until recently, many of us were taught to see God as unapproachable and far away. Now we are realizing that the Infinite Intelligence that governs all of creation is also in us. The presence we have been searching for outside ourselves is actually a part of our own consciousness.

According to an ancient legend, the gods decided to hide man's divinity in a place where he would not find it. "Here is what we will do with man's divinity," they said. "We will hide it deep within man himself, for that is the last place he would ever think to look for it."

It is time for each of us to retrieve that lost divinity, to look within and touch that source that has been there all along. The love you experience will tell you that you have come home.

Heaven is here. There is nowhere else.
Heaven is now. There is no other time.
A Course in Miracles

Without going out of his door,
one can know the universe.
Without looking out his window,
a man can perceive the heavenly Tao.
Lao-tzu

And when he was demanded of the Pharisees,
when the kingdom of God should come,
he answered them and said,
"The kingdom of God cometh not with observation:
Neither shall they say, Lo here! or, lo there!
for, behold,
the kingdom of God is within you."
Luke 17:20–21

Know ye not that ye are the temple of God,
and that the Spirit of God dwelleth in you?
I Corinthians 3:16

God was concealed as a diamond in my heart.
Sikh Proverb

I gazed into my heart.
There I saw Him; He was nowhere else.
Rumi

Though the good is near, men neither see nor hear it.
Golden Verses of the Pythagoreans

The wellspring of undiluted joy of spirit
is buried within your soul.
Discover it and bathe in that fountain of eternal bliss.
Paramahansa Yogananda

Paradise is nearer to you
than the thongs of your sandals.
The Koran

Are you looking for me? I am in the next seat.
My shoulder is against yours.
You will not find me in stupas, not in Indian shrine
rooms, nor in synagogues, nor in cathedrals;
not in masses nor kirtans,
not in legs winding around your own neck,
nor in eating nothing but vegetables.

When you really look for me,
you will see me instantly—
you will find me in the tiniest house of time.
Kabir says: Student, tell me, what is God?
He is the breath inside the breath.

Kabir

If God seems far away, who moved?
Alcoholics Anonymous

Depend more upon the intuitive forces from within and not harken so much to outside influences but learn to listen to the still small voice within.

Edgar Cayce

Guidance

When the prophet Elijah went to the mountaintop to receive divine guidance, he discovered that God dwelled not in the wind, the fire, or the earthquake but in "a still small voice" within. Today we also must attune to this inner voice to find the answers and guidance we seek.

How does one hear this voice of truth? The key is to quiet the mind and allow the inner wisdom to rise up from your depths. Your intuition will speak to you in any number of ways—through words, a bodily sensation, a gut feeling, a picture, or just a general sense about things.

In seeking inner guidance, it is important to discern between the voice of truth and the "false voice," also known as the voice of the ego. When you follow the true voice, your life will be filled with peace, clarity, joy, and assistance from the universe. The false voice brings the opposite—confusion and struggle. In this way, the universe gives you feedback as to whether or not you are aligning yourself with the Higher Will.

Be still, and know that I am God.
Psalm 46:10

Let us become silent
that we may hear the whispers of the gods. . . .
There is guidance for each of us,
and by lowly listening we shall hear the right word.
Ralph Waldo Emerson

In a dream, in a vision of the night,
when deep sleep falleth upon men,
in slumberings upon the bed;
Then he openeth the ears of men, and
sealeth their instruction.
Job 33:15–16

If a man does not keep pace with his companions,
perhaps it is because he hears a different drummer.
Let him step to the music which he hears,
however measured or far away.
Henry David Thoreau

Never be afraid to tread the path alone.
Know which is your path and follow it
wherever it may lead you.
Eileen Caddy

Be a lamp unto yourself.
Hold to the truth within yourself.
Buddha

Trust in the Lord with all thine heart. . . .
In all thy ways acknowledge him,
and he shall direct thy paths.
Proverbs 3:5–6

Let nothing disturb thee, nothing afright thee;
All things are passing, God never changes.
Patient endurance attaineth to all things.
Who God possesses in nothing is wanting;
Alone God suffices.
St. Theresa of Avila

I will step back and let Him lead the way.
A Course in Miracles

When the internal eye is opened,
God who is the object of search and longing
is actually sighted.
Meher Baba

Stop talking, stop thinking,
and there is nothing you will not understand.
Return to the root and you will find the meaning;
Pursue the light and you lose its source.
Look inward, and in a flash you will conquer
the apparent and the void.
All come from mistaken views.
There is no need to seek the truth,
only stop having views.
Seng T'san

Close your eyes and you will see clearly.
Cease to listen and you will hear truth.
Be silent and your heart will sing.
Seek no contacts and you will find union.

Lao-tzu

❦

Faith

When following the spiritual path, one must deal with the experience of uncertainty. The future is not neatly planned or laid out; there are no guarantees. Feeling this insecurity, the conscious mind wants to know how life will unfold.

This is where faith takes over. With evidence lacking, we nevertheless step out in faith. And as the universe supports us again and again, we begin to feel comfortable living by faith—our "invisible means of support."

So make the decision to let go of worry, anxiety, and doubt and to trust in the process. Assistance will come; your needs will be met. The universe will not abandon you if you do not abandon your connection to it. Keep the faith, and the faith will keep you.

Now faith is the substance of things hoped for,
the evidence of things not seen.
Hebrews 11:1

When you come to the edge of all that you have known,
one of two things will happen.
Either you will step onto solid ground
or you will learn how to fly.
Anonymous

I am a man of faith. My reliance is solely on God.
One step is enough for me. The next step He will show
me when the time for it comes.
Gandhi

For we are saved by hope; but hope that is seen is not
hope: for what a man seeth, why doth he yet hope for?
But if we hope for that we see not,
then do we with patience wait for it.
Romans 8:24–25

Trust in God. Believe that He who created you
will maintain you.
Paramahansa Yogananda

The just shall live by his faith.
Habakkuk 2:4

*That faith is of little value which can
flourish only in fair weather.
Faith in order to be of any value
must survive the severest of trials.*
Gandhi

There are no atheists in foxholes.
Alcoholics Anonymous

*Faith is the bird that feels the light
and sings while the dawn is still dark.*
Cancer Survivor

If I have knowledge and resolute faith,
I shall walk in the Great Tao.
Lao-tzu

If ye have faith as a grain of mustard seed,
ye shall say unto this mountain,
"Remove hence to yonder place"; and it shall remove;
and nothing shall be impossible unto you.
Matthew 17:20

Understanding is the reward of faith.
Therefore seek not to understand
that thou mayest believe, but
believe that thou mayest understand.
St. Augustine

The only limits to our realization of tomorrow
will be our doubts of today.
Let us move forward with strong and active faith.
Franklin Delano Roosevelt

I have fought a good fight, I have finished my course,
I have kept the faith.
II Timothy 4:7

Truth

There once was a wise teacher who gave each of two men a chicken and told them to kill the chickens where no one would see them. The first man went behind the barn and killed his chicken. The second returned after three days with his chicken intact.

"Why didn't you kill the chicken?" the teacher asked. The man replied, "You told me to go where no one was looking, but everywhere I go, the chicken sees." It is the same in our lives: We can deceive others and even our own minds, but everywhere we go our own God-self sees.

Truth is what the spiritual quest is all about. Telling the truth to ourselves frees us from our self-imposed limitations. When you face the truth of a problem in your life, you can do something about it. Truth liberates, heals, and transforms. Resolve, therefore, to take that which is hidden in darkness and shine upon it the light of truth.

For me, God and truth are convertible terms.
Devotion to the truth is the sole reason
for our existence.
Gandhi

We must be true inside, true to ourselves,
before we can know a truth that is outside of us.
Thomas Merton

Ye shall know the truth,
and the truth shall make you free.
John 8:32

*The intoxication of life's pleasures and occupations
veils the Truth from men's eyes.*
Rumi

*The brilliant passes, like the dew at morn.
The truth endures, for ages yet unborn.*
Goethe

*Opinion is a flitting thing,
But truth outlasts the Sun—
If then we cannot own them both,
Possess the oldest one.*
Emily Dickinson

You may fool all the people some of the time;
you can even fool some of the people all of the time;
but you can't fool all of the people all of the time.
Abraham Lincoln

Oh, what a tangled web we weave,
When first we practice to deceive!
Sir Walter Scott

We are only as sick as our secrets.
Alcoholics Anonymous

This is Truth
But intellect cannot grasp it,
Wisdom cannot weigh it,
Space cannot hold it,
Angels cannot fathom it,
Time cannot check it,
but human beings can realize it
through Divine love, the love for the Almighty,
except for whom, nothing is.
Meher Baba

Rather than love, than money, than fame,
give me truth.
Henry David Thoreau

Truth is within ourselves; it takes no rise
From outward things what'er you may believe.
There is an inmost center in us all,
Where truth abides in fullness; and around,
Wall upon wall, the gross flesh hems it in,
This perfect, clear perception—which is truth.
A baffling and perverting carnal mesh
Binds it, and makes all error; and to know
Rather consists in opening out a way
Whence the imprisoned splendor may escape,
Than in effecting entry for a light
Supposed to be without.
Robert Browning

Thy Will Be Done

When we turn within and seek guidance, we find two voices clamoring for our attention—the voice of God and the voice of the ego. Following the divine voice brings peace and joy; pursuing the path of self creates anxiety and separation.

It is not always easy to choose the Higher Will; often we have to give up that which the ego holds most dear. But as we release our attachments, we are reborn to a larger reality where true happiness and peace abound.

This is why spiritual seekers have always affirmed: "Not my will, but thine, be done." State your willingness to let that Higher Power work through you for the highest good of yourself and others. Meditating on the following words will help you to attain this goal: "The Lord makes known His will to me, and I joyfully obey. Spirit guides my every step and love reveals the way."

*A little consideration of what takes place
around us every day would show us
that a higher law than that of our will regulates events.*
Ralph Waldo Emerson

*To say, "I of myself can do nothing"
is to gain all power. . . .
When this power is experienced,
it is impossible to trust one's petty strength again.
Who would attempt to fly with the wings of a sparrow
when the mighty power of an eagle has been given him?*
A Course in Miracles

The steps of a good man are ordered by the Lord:
and He delighteth in his way.
Psalm 37:23

There were those individuals in every age and generation
who were willing to say,
"I will be obedient to a higher law."
Martin Luther King, Jr.

WILLPOWER—
Our willingness to be used by a Higher Power.
Alcoholics Anonymous

Thy kingdom come. Thy will be done
in earth, as it is in heaven.
The Lord's Prayer

O my Father, if it be possible, let this cup pass from
me: nevertheless not as I will, but as thou wilt.
Matthew 26:39

Why art thou troubled because things do not succeed
according to thy desire?
Who is there who hath all things according to his will?
Neither I, nor thou, nor any man on earth.
Thomas à Kempis

That wonderful sense that I'm not doing it, that I'm outside my ego and am surrendering my instrumentality to that power that is coming through me; that is of course the best gift a person can get from his tradition.
Rabbi Zalman Schacter

Repeat three times every day and then listen: "Lord, what would thou have me do today?"
Edgar Cayce

It is not wrong to tell the Lord that we want something, but it shows greater faith if we simply say, "Heavenly Father. I know that thou dost anticipate my every need. Sustain me according to Thy will."
Paramahansa Yogananda

I asked for bread and got a stone;
I used the stone to grind the grain
That made the flour
To form the bread
That I could not obtain.

Instead of asking Him to give
The things for which we pray,
All that we need to ask
From God is this:
Show us the way.
James Bowman

The Blessing of Giving

Many great philosophies state that it is better to give than to receive. This statement is more than a platitude. You can feel its truth in your heart whenever you freely give of yourself.

True prosperity comes not from one's bank account or investments but from the joy of sharing. In the film *It's a Wonderful Life*, George Bailey's service to his community generated such feelings of goodwill that the townspeople donated their own money to pay off a large debt that threatened to wipe out his business. To this gesture Bailey responded, "No man can be called poor who has friends."

The paradox is clear: What you give out comes back. What you give away is yours to keep. All that you give you give to yourself.

All who joy would win
Must share it,—happiness was born a twin.
Lord Byron

And there are those who have little and give it all.
They are the believers in life and the bounty of life,
and their coffer is never empty.
Kahlil Gibran

It is one of the most beautiful compensations of this life
that no man can sincerely try to help another
without also helping himself.
Ralph Waldo Emerson

It is more blessed to give than to receive.
Acts 20:35

Cast thy bread upon the waters:
for thou shalt find it after many days.
Ecclesiastes 11:1

A man there was, tho' some did count him mad,
The more he cast away, the more he had.
John Bunyan

Lay not up for yourselves treasures upon earth,
where moth and rust doth corrupt,
and where thieves break through and steal:
But lay up for yourselves treasures in heaven. . . .
For where your treasure is,
there will your heart be also.
Matthew 6:19–21

The wise man does not lay up treasure;
his riches are within.
The more he gives to others,
the more he has of his own.
Lao-tzu

Goodness is the only investment that never fails.
Henry David Thoreau

Money should always be kept in circulation.
If you hoard it for a rainy day,
you'll have to spend it on an ark.
Proverb

There is that scattereth, and yet increaseth;
and there is that withholdeth more than is meet,
but it tendeth to poverty.
Proverbs 11:24

The greatest gift is a portion of thyself.
Ralph Waldo Emerson

So let him give; not grudgingly, or of necessity:
for God loveth a cheerful giver.
II Corinthians 9:7

To give and then not feel that one has given
is the very best of all ways of giving.
Max Beerbohm

Oneness

We are all one. This oneness can be seen in a number of ways. The components of the DNA of all living organisms are identical. Despite outer physical differences, we are quite similar on a cellular level. The invention of the hologram shows that each part of the universe contains within it the imprint of the entire creation. Mind-body scientists are acknowledging what mystics have always known—that there exists one "collective mind" that links the consciousness of all living things.

Although the ego continues to believe in the illusion of separateness, a deeper wisdom knows that we are one. Experience your oneness with all of creation. Such feelings of unity will lead you directly to the realization of divine love.

A human being is part of the whole called by us a
universe—a part limited in time and space. He
experiences himself, his thoughts and his feelings, as
something separate from the rest, a kind of optical
delusion of his consciousness.

This delusion is a kind of prison for us; it restricts
us to our personal decisions and our affections to a few
persons nearest to us.

Our task must be to free ourselves from this prison
by widening our circle of compassion to embrace all
living creatures and the whole of nature in its beauty.

Albert Einstein

The unity that binds us together,
that makes this earth a family
and all men brothers and sons of God, is love.

Thomas Wolfe

Religions are different roads
converging upon the same point.
What does it matter that we take different roads
so long as we reach the same goal?
Gandhi

A universal theology is impossible.
But a universal experience is not only possible
but necessary.
A Course in Miracles

Have we not all one father?
hath not one God created us?
Malachi 2:10

Whether I am conscious of it or not,
I am one with the cause of all that exists.
Whether I feel it or not, I am one
with all the love in the universe.
Thaddeus Golas

Thou canst not stir a flower
without troubling of a star.
Francis Thompson

To see a World in a Grain of Sand,
And a Heaven in a Wild Flower,
Hold Infinity in the palm of your hand,
And Eternity in an hour.
William Blake

All are but parts of one stupendous whole,
Whose body nature is, and God the soul.
Alexander Pope

Are not the mountains, waves, and skies a part
Of me and my soul, as I of them?
Lord Byron

Our cultural patterns are an amalgam
of black and white.
Our destinies are tied together.
None of us can make it alone.
Martin Luther King, Jr.

The universe is a perfect, undivided whole,
and healing can take place only when
one is unified with it.
Ernest Holmes

I am one with thee O Thou Infinite One.
I am where thou art.
I am what thou art.
I am because thou art.
Prayer for Union With God

Love Your Neighbor

Out of the consciousness of "oneness" comes the recognition of the oneness of humanity. Nonetheless, we mistakenly think that our interests are different from our neighbor's and act to oppose the so-called enemy.

But the division between "us" and "them" is a false one. Each individual is a cell in the body of humanity. If one part of the body is harmed, every other part experiences the pain. As the poet John Donne observed centuries ago, "Any man's death diminishes me, because I am involved in mankind."

The time has come for us to realize that we are more alike than different, that the love that joins us is more powerful than the fear that divides us. A new awareness of the oneness of humanity is being born. With this realization, we can rise above our apparent differences and affirm our commonality as brothers and sisters of one human family.

No man is an island, entire of itself;
every man is a piece of the continent,
a part of the main.
John Donne

By nature, men are nearly alike;
By practice, they get to be far apart.
Confucius

We must widen the circle of our love
until it embraces the whole village;
the village in turn must take into its fold
the district; the district the province, and so on till the
scope of our love encompasses the whole world.
Gandhi

Man must evolve for all human conflict
a method which rejects revenge, aggression, and
retaliation. The foundation of such a method is love.
Martin Luther King, Jr.

Whatsoever ye would that men should do to you,
do ye even so to them:
for this is the law and the prophets.
Matthew 7:12

What you do not want done to yourself,
do not do to others.
The Golden Rule of Confucianism

Today's problem is not atomic energy but man's heart.
Peace cannot be kept by force.
It can only be achieved by understanding.
Albert Einstein

In all the world there is no such thing as a stranger.
Japanese Proverb

When you meet people,
pretend that you already know them.
The Dalai Lama

This is my commandment, That ye love one another,
as I have loved you.
John 15:12

Do you love your Creator?
Then love your fellow beings first.
The Koran

To love God in the most practical way
is to love our fellow human beings.
If we feel for others in the same way as we feel
for our dear ones, we love God.
Meher Baba

To those who are good to me I am good.
To those who are not good to me I am good also.
Thus all get to be good.
Lao-tzu

But I say unto you which hear, Love your enemies,
do good to them which hate you,
Bless them that curse you, and pray for them
which despitefully use you.
Luke 6:27–28

No act of kindness, however small, is ever wasted.
Aesop's Fables

Service

One of the keys to spiritual growth is loving service. In Eastern traditions, karma yoga, or the path of "right action," is a method by which one can achieve enlightenment.

Like the law of giving, the desire to serve is based on the awareness that we are all part of one human family. I cannot feel at peace if my brother or sister is in pain.

This is the realization of the "bodhisattva," the person who, after achieving his own enlightenment, chooses to share his light with others who are still suffering. Like him, each of us knows that when we serve others, we are also serving ourselves.

Choose you this day whom ye will serve . . .
but as for me and my house, we will serve the Lord.
Joshua 24:15

I don't know what your destiny will be,
but one thing I do know:
The only ones among you who will be really happy
are those who will have sought and found how to serve.
Albert Schweitzer

I slept and dreamt that life was joy.
I awoke and saw that life was service.
I acted and behold! service was joy.
Tagore

I sought my soul, but my soul I could not see.
I sought my God, but my God eluded me.
I sought my brother and I found all three.
Anonymous

The wise devote themselves to the welfare of all,
for they see themselves in all.
Upanishads

For whosoever will save his life shall lose it:
and whosoever will lose his life for my sake shall find it.
Matthew 16:25

To leave the world a little bit better,
whether by a healthy child, a garden patch,
or a redeemed social condition;
To know that even one life has breathed easier
because you have lived:
This is to have succeeded.
Thomas Stanley

The highest reward for a person's toil
is not what they get for it
but what they become by it.
John Ruskin

We cannot live only for ourselves.
A thousand fibers connect us with our fellow humans.
Herman Melville

For I was hungered, and ye gave me meat:
I was thirsty, and ye gave me drink:
I was a stranger, and ye took me in:
Naked, and ye clothed me:
I was sick, and ye visited me:
I was in prison, and ye came unto me.
Matthew 25:35–36

The highest worship of God is service to man.
Andrew Carnegie

Know that the purpose for which each soul enters a
material experience is that it may be
as a light unto others.
Edgar Cayce

If I can help somebody as I pass along,
If I can cheer somebody with a word or song,
If I can show somebody he's traveling wrong,
Then my living will not be in vain.

If I can do my duty as a Christian ought,
If I can bring salvation to a world once wrought,
If I can spread the message as the master taught,
Then my living will not be in vain.

Yes, Jesus, I want to be on your right or your left side,
not for any selfish reason.
I want to be on your right or your left side,
not in terms of some political kingdom or ambition.

But I just want to be there,
in love and in justice and in truth and
in commitment to others,
so that we can make of this old world a new world.
Martin Luther King, Jr.
(excerpted from the Drum Major Sermon)

Love Yourself

We have spoken of one's relationship with God and one's relationship to others. There exists a third relationship that is equally significant—the relationship you have with yourself.

You are a child of the universe, "fearfully and wonderfully made." In the history of creation, there has never been anyone like you. Accept this reality about yourself—that you are a special, unique human being who has a place on this earth that no one else can fill.

Acknowledge yourself as a glorious expression of your loving Creator. This healthy self-love will form the foundation of a joyful and satisfying life. Then, as you love and accept yourself, your inner light will shine outward to bless and heal your fellow human beings.

Whatever you are doing, love yourself for doing it.
Whatever you are feeling, love yourself for feeling it.
Thaddeus Golas

If I am not for myself, who will be for me?
Hillel

You must love yourself before you love another.
By accepting yourself and fully being what you are,
your simple presence can make others happy.
Jane Roberts

To love oneself is the beginning of a lifelong romance.
Oscar Wilde

I celebrate myself, and sing myself . . .
I am larger, better than I thought,
I did not know I held so much goodness.
Walt Whitman

I think the greatest victory of this period
was something internal.
The greatest victory of this period was that we
armed ourselves with dignity and self-respect.
Martin Luther King, Jr.

It is easy to live for others. Everybody does.
I call on you to live for yourselves.
Ralph Waldo Emerson

A man cannot be comfortable
without his own approval.
Mark Twain

It is difficult to make a man miserable
while he feels worthy of himself
and claims kindred to the great God who made him.
Abraham Lincoln

"It is beautiful to think that the Lord loves us all equally," a visitor said. "But it seems unjust that he should care for a sinner as much as a saint."

"Is a diamond less valuable because it is covered with mud?" the Master answered. "God sees the changeless beauty of our souls. He knows we are not our mistakes."

Paramahansa Yogananda

Teach only love, for that is what you are.
A Course in Miracles

❦

Forgiveness

A truly divine attribute is that of forgiveness. Instead of following the old law—an eye for an eye, a tooth for a tooth—forgiveness counters evil with good, thereby transmuting wrongdoing by the higher alchemy of love. Thus, Jesus told his disciples, "Love your enemies."

Forgiveness arises when we can put ourselves in another's place and see things from his perspective. We realize that no matter how insensitive his actions seemed, he was doing the best he could with the awareness he had at the time. We can also gain perspective by realizing how often we need to be forgiven for our own mistakes.

Forgiveness is freeing—for yourself as well as for others. It frees you from carrying the burden of past resentments. It lets you release the past so that your energy can be fully available for the present. Forgiveness is the ultimate gift you can give to yourself.

Love truth, but pardon error.
Voltaire

The quality of mercy is not strain'd,
It droppeth as the gentle rain from heaven.
Shakespeare

Then Peter came to him, and said,
"Lord, how oft shall my brother sin against me,
and I forgive him? till seven times?"
Jesus saith unto him, "I say not unto thee,
Until seven times:
but, Until seventy times seven."
Matthew 18:21–22

Do what you do with another person;
but never put them out of your heart.
The Dalai Lama

It's really a wonder that I haven't dropped all my ideals,
because they seem so absurd and
impossible to carry out.
Yet, I keep them, because in spite of everything,
I still believe that people are really good at heart.
Anne Frank

Father, forgive them; for they know not what they do.
Luke 23:34

The old law of "an eye for an eye"
leaves everybody blind.
Martin Luther King, Jr.

Hatred is not diminished by hatred at any time.
Hatred is diminished by love. This is an eternal law.
Buddha

Forgiveness to the injured does belong;
But they ne'er pardon who have done the wrong.
John Dryden

To err is human, to forgive divine.
Alexander Pope

Out beyond ideas of wrongdoing and rightdoing,
there is a field. I'll meet you there.
Rumi

Always forgive your enemies—
nothing annoys them so much.
Oscar Wilde

If we could read the secret history of our enemies,
we should find in each man's life sorrow and suffering
enough to disarm all hostility.
Henry Wadsworth Longfellow

When you are offended at any man's fault, turn to
yourself and study your own failings.
Then you will forget your anger.
Epictetus

I will forgive all things today.
A Course in Miracles

Suffering

Pain is part of life. The first noble truth of Buddha states that life is suffering. Before leaving his disciples, Jesus said, "In the world ye shall have tribulation."

Suffering is not necessarily a bad thing. Pain is often the stimulus that brings spiritual growth and transformation. Sorrow can enhance our compassion and open us to a larger reality. A broken heart can become an open heart. The type of suffering that expands awareness is called *intentional* or *authentic* suffering.

Another kind of suffering is *neurotic* or *inauthentic* suffering. Neurotic suffering occurs when we run from our pain, see ourselves as victims, or choose not to forgive. Neurotic suffering does not serve us but keeps us stuck in unnecessary pain.

When suffering enters your life, you can use it to grow spiritually—or remain victimized by it. In this choice your real freedom lies.

There are places in the heart that do not yet exist.
Pain must be in order that they be.
Léon Bloy

Your pain is the breaking of the shell
that encloses your understanding.
Kahlil Gibran

Hearts live by being wounded.
Oscar Wilde

People have a need to feel their pain. Very often
pain is the beginning of a great deal of awareness.
As an energy center, it awakens consciousness.
Arnold Mindell

The only way out is through.
The only way to heal the pain is to embrace the pain.
Fritz Perls

We are healed of a suffering
only by experiencing it to the full.
Marcel Proust

*The one thing that distinguishes man from
the rest of the animal kingdom
is his capacity to suffer.*
Dostoyevsky

*Although the world is full of suffering,
it is also full of the overcoming of it.*
Helen Keller

He who has a why to live can bear almost any how.
Nietzsche

Don't grieve.
Anything you lose comes round in another form.
The child weaned from mother's milk
now drinks wine and honey mixed.
Rumi

Blessed are they that mourn:
for they shall be comforted.
Matthew 5:4

If you are distressed by anything external,
the pain is not due to the thing itself
but to your own estimate of it;
and this you have the power to revoke at any moment.
Marcus Aurelius

Into each life some rain must fall,
Some days must be dark and dreary.
Henry Wadsworth Longfellow

With all its sham, drudgery and broken dreams,
it is still a beautiful world.
Be cheerful. Strive to be happy.
Desiderata

Turning Trials Into Blessings

John Lennon once said, "Life is what happens to us when we are busy making other plans." As you travel the spiritual path, you will encounter your share of trials and tests. Often these difficulties may not seem to be a direct result of anything you did or caused. And while it is natural to ask, "Why me?" thinking of yourself as a victim can leave you feeling helpless and powerless.

To use adversity as a stimulus for growth, one can ask, "Now that I am facing this challenge, how can I respond in the most empowering way possible? How can I take this unwanted detour and use it as an opportunity to grow and to transform?"

When difficulties are faced in this way, miracles happen. Uninvited situations bring life-changing lessons. What began as an apparent misfortune emerges as a divine blessing. Such are the glorious and mysterious gifts that are bestowed upon us when we look for the good in the midst of adversity.

Sweet are the uses of adversity,
Which, like the toad, ugly and venomous,
Wears yet a precious jewel in his head;
And this our life, exempt from public haunt,
Finds tongues in trees, books in the running brooks,
Sermons in stones, and good in everything.
I would not change it.
Shakespeare

In life, the difficult periods are the best periods to gain
experience and shore up determination. As a result, my
mental status is much improved because of them.
The Dalai Lama

That which hurts also instructs.
Benjamin Franklin

A gem is not polished without rubbing
nor a man perfected without trials.
Confucius

Once you fully appreciate the vacuity
of a life without struggle,
you are equipped with the basic means of salvation.
Eugene O'Neill

Whom the Lord loveth he chasteneth.
Hebrews 12:6

When written in Chinese, the word "crisis"
is composed of two characters.
One represents danger
and the other represents opportunity.
John F. Kennedy
(from a speech given April 12, 1959)

Every adversity contains within it the seed
of an equivalent or greater good.
Princes of Serendip

Adversity is not necessarily evil.
Beethoven, after all, composed his greatest music when
he was deaf. Never give up!
Robert McCracken

*The ultimate measure of a man is not where he stands
in moments of comfort and convenience, but where
he stands at times of challenge and controversy.*
Martin Luther King, Jr.

*The depth of darkness to which you can descend
and still live is an exact measure of the height
that you can aspire to reach.*
Laurens Van der Post

What doesn't kill me makes me stronger.
Nietzsche

When one door of happiness closes another door opens;
but often we look so long at the closed door
that we do not see the one that has been opened for us.
Helen Keller

There is no such thing as a problem
without a gift for you in its hands. You seek problems
because you need their gifts.
Richard Bach

Kites fly highest against the wind, not with it.
Winston Churchill

We, ignorant of ourselves,
Beg often our own harms,
which the wise powers
Deny us for our good; so we find profit
By losing of our prayers.
Shakespeare

The worst thing that happened to me
was the best thing that happened to me.
My bad luck turned out to be my good luck.
Anonymous

Man's extremity is God's opportunity.
Alcoholics Anonymous

Difficulties meet us at every turn. They are the accompaniment of life. Out of pain grow the violets of patience and sweetness. The richness of the human experience would lose something of rewarding joy if there were no limitations to overcome.

Helen Keller

*But he knoweth the way that I take:
when he hath tried me, I shall come forth as gold.*

Job 23:10

Be not "sat upon" by disappointments. It is he who gets up each time that the Lord loves and will sustain.

Edgar Cayce

Patience

Worthwhile accomplishments do not occur overnight. They require time and patience—elements that enter into the great handiworks of man and nature.

The farmer does not plant his corn today and harvest it tomorrow. He must wait a season. Likewise, your good is also coming in *its* season. Sometimes we want the universe to operate on *our* time schedule, and we get upset if our plans are delayed. But often we are not as ready as we think, and the extra time can be used for additional preparation.

Patience can also help us to make it through the difficult times when challenges *seem* like they will go on forever. When you start to lose hope, realize that nothing lasts forever—that the current cycle will end and a new one will begin. Be patient. Spirit is on your side. It is only a matter of time until all will be healed.

They that wait upon the Lord shall renew their strength;
they shall mount up with wings as eagles;
they shall run, and not be weary;
and they shall walk, and not faint.
Isaiah 40:31

Allah is with those who patiently endure.
The Koran

They also serve who only stand and wait.
John Milton

Do not expect a spiritual blossom every day
in the garden of your life.
Have faith that the Lord to whom you have surrendered
will bring you Divine fulfillment at the proper time.
Paramahansa Yogananda

To every thing there is a season,
and a time to every purpose under the heaven.
Ecclesiastes 3:1

In due season we shall reap, if we faint not.
Galatians 6:9

Serene, I fold my hands and wait,
Nor care for wind, nor tide, nor sea;
I rave no more 'gainst time or fate,
For lo! my own shall come to me.
John Burroughs

How poor are they that have not patience!
What wound did ever heal but by degrees?
Shakespeare

Time is the great physician.
Benjamin Disraeli

Observe how the ant-hill grows, adding little to little.
Hindu Proverb

Rome was not built in one day.
John Heywood

Impatience with little things
makes confusion in great plans.
Confucius

Le genie c'est la patience.
Genius is patience.
Georges-Louis Leclerc

PATIENCE

Patience and diligence, like faith, remove mountains.
William Penn

Only with winter-patience can we bring;
the deep-desired, long-awaited spring.
Anne Morrow Lindbergh

Cheer up, Watson. Sea air, sunshine, patience—
All will be revealed.
Sherlock Holmes

Overcoming Fear

A major stumbling block in our quest for spiritual awareness is fear. Living in fear closes the heart, shuts down the intuition, and blocks our channel to the abundance of the universe.

In some instances (e.g., when danger is present), it is appropriate to be afraid. But many of our fears are self-created. These fears come in many guises—fear of poverty, fear of criticism, fear of failure, fear of death. Underlying them is the belief that we can be separate from our Source; yet it is not possible to be apart from the consciousness that created us.

When you feel overcome by any of these false fears, remember that they have no power over you. If you keep your focus on that benevolent Higher Power, your protection is assured. As the apostle Paul said, "If God be for us, who can be against us?"

*Fear is the main source of superstition, and one of the
main sources of cruelty.
To conquer fear is the beginning of wisdom.*
Bertrand Russell

*The Lord is my light and my salvation;
whom shall I fear?*
Psalm 27:1

*God is our refuge and strength,
a very present help in trouble.
Therefore will we not fear,
though the earth be removed,
and though the mountains be carried
into the midst of the sea.*
Psalm 46:1–2

Why should I fear Death's call? Can there e'er be
In life a more beautiful adventure than
To re-embark upon that unknown sea?
James Terry White

It seems to me most strange that men should fear;
Seeing that death, a necessary end,
Will come when it will come.
Shakespeare

A stone I died and rose again a plant,
A plant I died and rose an animal;
I died an animal and was born a man.
Why should I fear? What have I lost by death?
Rumi

No passion so effectively robs the mind of all its powers
of acting and reasoning as fear.
Edmund Burke

Fear is the darkroom where negatives are developed.
Alcoholics Anonymous

He who fears he will suffer
already suffers from his fear.
Montaigne

Fear knocked at the door.
Faith answered.
No one was there.
Hindu Proverb

Face the thing you fear,
and you do away with that fear.
Ralph Waldo Emerson

The only thing we have to fear is fear itself.
Franklin Delano Roosevelt

Have no fear of moving into the unknown.
Step out fearlessly, knowing that I am with you and
therefore no harm can befall you.
Eileen Caddy

Peace I leave with you, my peace I give unto you:
not as the world giveth, give I unto you.
Let not your heart be troubled, neither let it be afraid.
John 14:27

For God hath not given us the spirit of fear;
but of power, and of love, and of a sound mind.
II Timothy 1:7

There is no fear in love;
but perfect love casteth out fear.
I John 4:18

I will fear no evil: for thou art with me;
thy rod and thy staff they comfort me.
Psalm 23:4

Courage is resistance to fear, mastery of fear—
not absence of fear.
Mark Twain

Feel the fear and do it anyway.
Susan Jeffers

Let me not pray to be sheltered from the dangers,
but to be fearless in facing them.
Let me not beg for the stilling of my pain,
but for the heart to conquer it.
Let me not look for allies in life's battlefield,
but to my own strength.
Let me not crave in anxious fear to be saved,
but hope for the patience to win my freedom.
Tagore

Life only demands from you the strength you possess.
Only one feat is possible—not to have run away.
Dag Hammarskjöld

Just for today I will be unafraid.
Al-Anon

Divine Protection

Although we may not be aware of it, we are
surrounded by divine protection. In the midst of difficulty
or danger, we can call upon spirit to assist and protect
us. Under the guidance of this energy, we are protected
from harm or negativity in the outer world.

Recall those times in your life when you
experienced protection. Perhaps you narrowly escaped
having a major accident, or you were lifted out of an
impossible situation. In these cases, an invisible presence
kept you safe.

Each day, in prayer or meditation, dwell in that
God-consciousness at the center of your being. In that
quiet place, you will be lifted into the light where outer
disturbances cannot reach you. The quotations, prayers,
and invocations that follow will also bring forth that
inner protection that is your divine birthright.

❦

The Lord is my shepherd; I shall not want.
He maketh me to lie down in green pastures:
he leadeth me beside the still waters.
He restoreth my soul: he leadeth me in the paths of
righteousness for his name's sake. Yea, though I walk
through the valley of the shadow of death,
I will fear no evil: for thou art with me;
thy rod and thy staff they comfort me.
Thou preparest a table before me in the presence of
mine enemies: thou anointest my head with oil;
my cup runneth over.
Surely goodness and mercy shall follow me
all the days of my life:
and I will dwell in the house of the Lord for ever.

Psalm 23

May the long time sun shine upon you
All love surround you
And the pure light within you
Guide your way on.
Irish Blessing

The will of God will never take you where
the grace of God will not protect you.
Alcoholics Anonymous

If God be for us, who can be against us?
Romans 8:31

*The Lord shall preserve thy going out and thy coming in
from this time forth, and even for evermore.*
Psalm 121:8

*He that dwelleth in the secret place of the most High
shall abide under the shadow of the Almighty.
I will say of the Lord, He is my refuge and my
fortress: my God; in him will I trust. . . .
Because thou hast made the Lord, . . . thy habitation;
There shall no evil befall thee, neither shall any plague
come nigh thy dwelling.*
Psalm 91:1–2, 9–10

*The great blessing of the Spirit pours through me now
and protects me in all my ways.*
Ernest Holmes

The light of God surrounds me;
The love of God enfolds me;
The power of God protects me;
The presence of God watches over me.
Wherever I am, God is.
Prayer of Protection

I clothe myself in a robe of Light,
composed of the Love and the Power
and the Wisdom of God;
not only for my own protection,
but so that all who see it or come in contact with it
may be drawn to God and healed.
Use me Mother / Father God to the utmost capacity
for the coming of Thy kingdom on earth. Amen.
Robe of Light Prayer

God never forsakes us.
Silently he works in every way
to help his beloved children
and to hasten their spiritual progress.
Paramahansa Yogananda

Though he fall, he shall not be utterly cast down:
for the Lord upholdeth him with his hand.
Psalm 37:24

The winds of grace are blowing all the time.
You have only to raise your sail.
Ramakrishna

Healing

The word *healing* comes from the same root as the word *whole*. To be healed is to be made whole and complete, not lacking in any way.

Ask yourself, "Where do I need to be healed? Where do I need to seek wholeness?"

To nurture the body, give it proper nutrition, rest, and exercise.

To heal the mind, focus on uplifting thoughts of truth, love, and beauty.

Forgiveness is the key to emotional healing. Make peace with all those who have wronged you and forgive yourself for your own mistakes.

And to heal the spirit, find a way to commune with God "as you understand Him to be." Make that connection in the way that feels right to you, and a deep peace will fill your soul. Once you drink from the waters of the living spirit, you will never thirst again.

The most divine art is that of healing.
And if the healing art is most divine, it must occupy
itself with the soul as well as the body; for no creature
can be sound so long as the higher part of it is suffering.
Pythagoras

Of the most High cometh healing.
Ecclesiastes

Daughter, thy faith hath made thee whole.
Mark 5:34

This is the day when healing comes to us.
This is the day when separation ends,
and we remember Who we really are.
A Course in Miracles

Healing takes place as our minds become attuned
to the truth of our Being.
Ernest Holmes

Let the weak say, "I am strong."
Joel 3:10

*A sound mind in a sound body, is a short
but full description of a happy state in this world.*
John Locke

*The physician should know the invisible as well as
the visible man. There is a great difference between
the power which removes the invisible cause of disease
and that which merely causes
external effects to disappear.*
Paracelsus

*No permanent healing is possible if a person
continues to make the same mistake
and thus invites the return of the disease.*
Paramahansa Yogananda

I am still and know that I am a child of the healing power of the universe. It flows through me and into ____ (name of person) to heal, renew, restore, and make well, healthy and whole, anything in his body, mind or soul that needs it.

The white light protects us, and I approach this person with love so that only the highest can come to either one of us. I let spirit direct my thoughts and actions to do what they need to do. The divine healing energy exchanged between us blesses us both for having come together today. Amen.

Maggie Kelley

(spoken prior to a healing treatment)

Deliverance

There is an old saying that God will never give you more than you can handle. No matter how difficult the situation or hopeless the outlook, a light always shines at the end of the tunnel. As the Psalmist wrote, "They that sow in tears shall reap in joy."

To bring about deliverance, start by doing all that you can to promote your own recovery. This includes reaching out to others for support. When you have done all that is humanly possible, then turn within and ask for assistance.

The Almighty has not forgotten you. Soon you will rise out of your ashes and spread your wings like a soaring eagle. And from that heightened perspective, you will see that all along invisible hands were guiding you safely home.

Many are the afflictions of the righteous:
but the Lord delivereth him out of them all.
Psalm 34:19

Sometimes I get discouraged and feel my work is in
vain. But then the Holy Spirit revives my soul again.
Martin Luther King, Jr.

I will turn their mourning into joy, and will comfort
them, and make them rejoice from their sorrow.
Jeremiah 31:13

In the depth of winter,
I finally learned that within me there lay
an invincible summer.
Albert Camus

For I reckon that the sufferings of this present time
are not worthy to be compared
with the glory which shall be revealed in us.
Romans 8:18

Enlightenment begins
on the other side of despair.
Jean-Paul Sartre

God is our refuge and strength,
a very present help in trouble.
Psalm 46:1

I see the world gradually being turned into a wilderness.
I can feel the suffering of millions and yet,
if I look up to the heavens, I think it will all come right,
that this cruelty too will end, and that peace and
tranquility will return again.
Anne Frank

God is never late.
Alcoholics Anonymous

When you do your work with the thought of serving
God, you receive his blessings.
So long as you work to please God,
all cosmic forces will harmoniously assist you.
Paramahansa Yogananda

Because he hath set his love upon me, therefore will I
deliver him: I will set him on high,
because he hath known my name.
Psalm 91:14

Don't give up five minutes before the miracle!
Alcoholics Anonymous

Transformation / Rebirth

"Except a man be born again, he cannot see the kingdom of God." This statement from the gospel of John describes the rebirth that initiates the journey on the spiritual path. It is a shift from self-centeredness to God-centeredness, from the ego to the higher self, from "my will" to "Thy will."

In a real sense, this shift from third-dimensional to fourth-dimensional consciousness parallels the Easter story of the crucifixion and resurrection. As we die to our human wants, attachments, and desires and let the knowing part of ourselves take over, we are reborn to our divine, eternal self.

Like physical birth, spiritual birth marks the beginning of a new life. One continues to live as before but sees the world with new eyes. As you undergo this rebirth, a new dimension of joy and peace will fill your being. Rest in this presence. This is the kingdom of heaven manifesting through you and as you.

We are born into the world of nature;
our second birth is into the world of spirit.
Bhagavad-Gita

Rebirth is triple;
there is firstly the rebirth of our intelligence;
secondly of our heart and our will;
and finally the rebirth of our entire being.
Karl von Eckarthshausen

Man's main task in life
is to give birth to himself,
to become what he potentially is.
Erich Fromm

Behold, I show you a mystery;
We shall not all sleep,
but we shall all be changed,
In a moment, in the twinkling of an eye,
at the last trump: for the trumpet shall sound,
and the dead shall be raised incorruptible,
and we shall be changed.
I Corinthians 15:51–52

To be a traveler on this earth,
you must know how to die and come to life again.
Goethe

A man who dies before he dies,
Does not die when he dies.
African Proverb

One discovers that destiny can be directed,
that one does not have to remain in bondage
to the first wax imprint made in childhood.
Once the deforming mirror is smashed, there is a
possibility of wholeness; there is a possibility of joy.
Anaïs Nin

And be not conformed to this world:
but be ye transformed by the renewing of your mind.
Romans 12:2

We surrender to win,
We die to live,
We suffer to get well,
We give it away to keep it.
Alcoholics Anonymous

*When you feel that you have reached the end
And that you cannot go one step further,
when life seems to be drained of all purpose,
what a wonderful opportunity to start all over again,
to turn over a new page.*
Eileen Caddy

*That men may rise on stepping-stones
Of their dead selves to higher things.*
Alfred, Lord Tennyson

*For this my son was dead, and is alive again;
he was lost, and is found.*
Luke 15:24

The people that walked in darkness
have seen a great light:
they that dwell in the land of the shadow of death,
upon them hath the light shined.
Isaiah 9:2

Well, I don't know what will happen now. We've
got some difficult days ahead. But it really doesn't
matter to me now. Because I've been to the
mountaintop. . . . And I've looked over, and I've seen
the Promised Land. I may not get there with you, but I
want you to know tonight that we as a people will get to
the Promised Land.

So I'm happy tonight. I'm not worried about
anything. I'm not fearing any man. Mine eyes have
seen the glory of the coming of the Lord!

Martin Luther King, Jr.
(spoken on the eve of his death)

Love

Love and life are inseparable from each other. Where there is life, there is love. Even on the most rudimentary level of consciousness, living things reach beyond their limitations and merge with other forms. Love is the attractive force that seeks this unity. It is the cosmic glue that holds the universe together.

We are told that "the kingdom of God is within you." Love is the key that gives us access to that inner kingdom and all of its riches.

"You shall love the Lord your God with all your heart, with all your soul, with all your strength, and with all your might, and your neighbor as yourself." This quotation shows there are three types of love—love for God, love for oneself, and love for another. Let us embody these dimensions of love so that we can experience the bliss and unity that come from experiencing life with an open heart.

Love is the willingness to extend oneself for the sake of nurturing one's own or another's spiritual growth.
M. Scott Peck

There is no path greater than love.
There is no law higher than love.
And there is no goal beyond love.
God and love are identical.
Meher Baba

It is only with the heart that one can see rightly;
what is essential is invisible to the eye.
Antoine de Saint-Exupéry

LOVE

Love alters not with his brief hours and weeks,
But bears it out even to the edge of doom.
If this be error, and upon me proved,
I never writ, nor no man ever loved.
Shakespeare

Love alone is capable of uniting living beings in such a
way as to complete and fulfill them, for it alone takes
them and joins them by what is deepest in themselves.
Teilhard de Chardin

When I ask our Lord to let me do something
for Him before I die, that
I may not appear before Him with empty hands,
He makes me understand that one act of love
gives Him greater glory than anything else.
T. Higginson

God's pure sweet love is not confined
By creeds which segregate and raise a wall.
His love enfolds, embraces human kind
No matter what ourselves or Him we call.
Then why not take Him at His word?
Why hold to creeds which tear apart?
But one thing matters, be it heard,
That brother love fill every heart.
There's but one thing the world has need to know,
There's but one balm for all our human woe:
There's but one way that leads to heaven above—
That way is human sympathy and love.
Max Heindell

Love is the highest and holiest action because it always
contains that which is not love within itself.
It always and ever moves to include the unloving.
Thaddeus Golas

LOVE

There is no difficulty that enough love will not conquer,
no disease that enough love will not heal;
no door that enough love will not open;
no gulf that enough love will not bridge;
no wall that enough love will not throw down;
no sin that enough love will not redeem. . . .
It makes no difference how deeply seated
may be the trouble; how hopeless the outlook;
how muddled the tangle; how great the mistake.
A sufficient realization of love will dissolve it all.
If only you could love enough you would be the happiest
and most powerful being in the world.

Emmet Fox

Love never fails.
I Corinthians 13:8

Though I speak with the tongues of men and angels but have not love, I have become as a sounding brass or a clanging cymbal.

And though I have the gift of prophecy, and understand all mysteries and all knowledge, and though I have all faith so that I could remove mountains, but have not love, I am nothing.

And though I bestow all my goods to feed the poor, and though I give my body to be burned, but have not love, it profits me nothing.

Love suffers long and is kind; love does not envy; love does not parade itself, is not puffed up; does not behave rudely, does not seek its own, is not provoked, thinks no evil;

Does not rejoice in iniquity but rejoices in the truth.

Bears all things, believes all things, hopes all things, endures all things.

Love never fails. But whether there are prophecies, they will fail; whether there are tongues, they will cease; whether there is knowledge, it will vanish away.

LOVE

❦

For we know in part and we prophesy in part.

But when that which is perfect has come, then that which is in part will be done away. . . .

And now abide faith, hope, love, these three; but the greatest of these is love.

I Corinthians 13

The night has a thousand eyes,
And the day but one;
Yet the light of the bright world dies
With the dying sun.
The mind has a thousand eyes,
And the heart but one;
Yet the light of a whole life dies
When love is done.

Francis Bourdillon

Through love, thorns become roses,
vinegar becomes sweet wine,
the stake becomes a thorn,
the reverse of fortune seems good fortune,
a prison becomes a rose bower,
a grate full of ashes seems a garden,
the devil becomes a houri,
the hard stone becomes soft as butter,
grief is as joy,
ghouls turn into angels,
stings are as honey,
lions are as harmless as mice,
sickness is as health,
wrath is as mercy.
Rumi

Inner Peace

A sure sign of the presence of spirit in one's life is the experience of inner peace. This peace is not a superficial or temporary peace. It is a "peace . . . which passeth all understanding" that emerges from a place deep in the soul.

Inner peace does not require the existence of harmonious circumstances in the outer world. Rather, it is a refuge from which you can literally rise above any turmoil or chaos that surrounds you.

The more you go inside and experience inner peace, the more it will be expressed in your outer life as peaceful actions. As other individuals join you and demonstrate lives of peace, so, too, will groups and nations. In this way, our common dream of world peace will become a reality.

INNER PEACE

Serenity is not freedom from the storm
but peace amid the storm.
Alcoholics Anonymous

Thou wilt keep him in perfect peace,
whose mind is stayed on thee.
Isaiah 26:3

Perfect bliss grows only in the heart made tranquil.
Hindu Proverb

Keep thyself first in peace,
and then thou wilt be able to bring others to peace.
Thomas à Kempis

Peace, like charity, begins at home.
Franklin Delano Roosevelt

We must come to see that peace
is not merely a distant goal that we seek,
but a means by which we arrive at that goal.
We must pursue peaceful ends through peaceful means.
Martin Luther King, Jr.

Lord, make me an instrument of Your peace.
Where there is hatred let me sow love;
where there is injury, pardon;
where there is doubt, faith;
where there is despair, hope;
where there is darkness, light; and
where there is sadness, joy.

O divine Master, grant that I may not so much seek
to be consoled as to console;
to be understood as to understand;
to be loved as to love.
For it is in giving that we receive;
it is in pardoning that we are pardoned;
and it is in dying that we are born to eternal life.
Prayer of St. Francis of Assisi

Nothing real can be threatened.
Nothing unreal exists.
Herein lies the peace of God.
A Course in Miracles

This is the way to inner peace:
Overcome evil with good, falsehood with truth,
and hatred with love.
Peace Pilgrim

Peace I leave with you, my peace I give unto you:
not as the world giveth, give I unto you.
John 14:27

Contentment makes poor men rich,
Discontent makes rich men poor.
Benjamin Franklin

If you lose your possessions, you've lost a lot.
If you lose your health, you've lost a great deal.
But if you lose your peace of mind,
you've lost everything.
Proverb

Peace of mind is my only goal.
A Course in Miracles

Let there be peace on earth
and let it begin with me.
Jill Jackson and Sy Miller

Peace is a chain reaction of love.
A First-grader

Blessed are the peacemakers:
for they shall be called the children of God.
Matthew 5:9

Tranquillity! thou better name
Than all the family of Fame.
Samuel Taylor Coleridge

My crown is called content;
A crown it is that seldom kings enjoy.
Shakespeare

❦

Abundance

Abundance is the natural state of the universe—of this there can be no doubt. Just as the number of stars in the heavens or drops of water in the ocean is beyond counting, so are the spiritual and material blessings that have been prepared for us.

The key to tapping into this abundance is to acknowledge God as your source. It is from the spiritual realm that all good comes to us. When we seek to connect with that source and act on its instructions, we automatically draw to us the people, resources, and circumstances that we need.

Just as a loving parent wishes to provide the best for his offspring, our loving Creator wishes His children to experience only health, happiness, success, and prosperity. Open yourself to receive this good that the universe longs to give you.

*What we need to realize above all else is that God has
provided for the most minute needs of our daily life, and
that if we lack anything it is because we have not made
contact with the supermind and the cosmic ray that
automatically flows from it.*
Charles Fillmore

*Fear not, little flock; for it is your Father's
good pleasure to give you the kingdom.*
Luke 12:32

The righteous shall flourish like the palm tree.
Psalm 92:12

*Prosperity is the outpicturing of substance
in all our affairs.
Everything in the universe is for us.
Nothing is against us. Life is giving of itself.*
Ernest Holmes

*Making money honestly and industriously
to serve God's work is the next greatest art after the
art of realizing God.*
Paramahansa Yogananda

*Wealth, properly employed, is a blessing; and one may
lawfully endeavor to increase it by honest means.*
The Koran

You can have prosperity no matter what your present circumstances may be. The Law gives you the power to attain prosperity and position without infringing upon the rights and opportunities of anyone else in the world.
Emmet Fox

Man was born to grow rich through the use of his faculties, by the union of thought and nature.
Ralph Waldo Emerson

My cup runneth over.
Psalm 23:5

Gratitude

The scriptural reason for expressing gratitude comes from the passage, "All things work together for good to them that love God." If this is true, then *all* experiences and circumstances in our lives are bringing us closer to truth. Every experience serves to make us more holy, and therefore everything is a blessing.

Essentially, there are two times to be thankful—when things are going well and when they are not going well. While it is easy to give thanks in the midst of plenty, it becomes more difficult in the midst of adversity. Why should we be grateful for the difficult times? Because a spiritual law tells us that every adversity contains within it the seed of an equivalent or greater good. Blessing the pain reveals this hidden good, and the difficulty turns into a wondrous blessing. Giving thanks is truly transforming.

Rejoice evermore. Pray without ceasing.
In every thing give thanks.
I Thessalonians 5:16 – 18

A thankful heart is not only the greatest virtue,
But the parent of all other virtues.
Cicero

When you learn to love hell, you will be in heaven.
Thaddeus Golas

So will I compass thine altar, O Lord:
That I may publish with the voice of thanksgiving,
and tell of all thy wondrous works.
Psalm 26:6–7

It's a pity we can't forget our troubles
the same way that we forget our blessings.
Alcoholics Anonymous

He is a wise man who does not grieve
for the things which he has not,
but rejoices for those he has.
Epictetus

God has two dwellings, one in heaven
and the other in a meek and thankful heart.
Izaak Walton

I will give thanks unto thee,
for I am fearfully and wonderfully made.
1662 Prayer Book

Gratitude is heaven itself.
William Blake

❦

Joy

Joy is the touchstone of the spiritual life. It is the emotion behind all other emotions. It is what lies at the core of us after we have cleared away the debris of our past conditioning and programming. Joy, therefore, is our natural state.

There are many ways to experience joy. Laughter brings about a lightness of the heart, as does playing with young children. Joy is linked to the creative process, as demonstrated by the joy that artists feel when they give birth to their creations. Can you imagine how much joy was expressed when the universe was created?

With the tests and challenges that compose this earth school, let us not forget the joy—the joy of being alive and experiencing the wonder and beauty of the universe. Surely this is reason to celebrate!

If life gave us at one time everything we wanted,
such as wealth, power and friends,
we would sooner or later become tired of them;
but there is one thing that can never become stale to us:
joy itself.
Paramahansa Yogananda

And my soul shall be joyful in the Lord.
Psalm 35:9

The greatest of God's angels is Joy.
She leans over us and gives us the secret of eternity,
which is Love.
I used to weep that all did not share.
Norman Lee

I certainly am a happy person.
How could one know God and not be joyous?
Peace Pilgrim

You pray in your distress and in your need;
would that you might pray also
in the fullness of your joy.
Kahlil Gibran

In bliss these creatures are born,
in bliss they are sustained,
and to bliss they merge again.
The Vedas

❦

And I have the firm belief in this now,
not only in terms of my own experience
but in knowing about the experience of others,
that when you follow your bliss, doors will open where
you would not have thought there were going to be
doors and where there wouldn't be a door
for anybody else.
Joseph Campbell

The gloom of the world is but a shadow.
Behind it, yet within its reach, is joy.
There is radiance and glory in the darkness
could we but see, and to see we have only to look.
I beseech you to look.
Fra Giovanni

JOY

What you call "salvation"
belongs to the time before death.
If you make love with the divine now, in the next life
you will have the face of satisfied desire.
Kabir

Take all away from me, but leave me Ecstasy,
And I am richer than all my fellow men.
Emily Dickinson

God respects me when I work,
but He loves me when I sing.
Tagore

❧

Simplicity

The essence of life is simplicity. The great truths of life—love, forgiveness, unity, giving—are simple. Likewise, realized masters and teachers are simple, unpretentious, and childlike.

It is a challenge not to be overwhelmed by the multitude of choices and options that are presented to us each day. The way out lies in focusing on what is truly essential.

Take a moment and ask yourself, "What are those simple activities—spending time with a good friend, taking a walk by the ocean, accomplishing a short-term goal—that bring me true peace and contentment? What steps can I take to reduce the clutter in my life so that I may live simply and joyously?"

As you begin to simplify your life, you will discover a new joy and freedom. It truly is a gift to be simple.

SIMPLICITY

'Tis a gift to be simple, 'Tis a gift to be free.
Shaker Hymn

Teach us delight in simple things,
And mirth that has no bitter springs.
Rudyard Kipling

We are not rich by what we possess
but rather by what we can do without.
Immanuel Kant

Live simply that others may simply live.
Anonymous

*The firm, the enduring, the simple, and the modest
are near to virtue.*
Confucius

*There is no greatness where there is not simplicity,
goodness and truth.*
Leo Tolstoy

Leave off that excessive desire of knowing;
therein is found much distraction.
There are many things the knowledge of which
is of little or no profit to the soul.
Thomas à Kempis

Manifest plainness,
Embrace simplicity,
Reduce selfishness,
Have few desires.
Lao-tzu

Our life is frittered away by detail . . .
Simplify, simplify.
Henry David Thoreau

I thank thee, O Father, Lord of heaven and earth,
because thou hast hid these things
from the wise and prudent,
and hast revealed them unto babes.
Matthew 11:25

And all the loveliest things there be
Come simply, so it seems to me.
Edna St. Vincent Millay

Simplicity, most rare in our age.
Ovid

Knowledge is acquired by daily gain:
but the Way is acquired by daily loss.
Lao-tzu

Besides the noble art of getting things done,
there is the noble art of leaving things undone.
The wisdom of life consists
in the elimination of nonessentials.
Lin Yutang

Less is more.
Robert Browning

The greatest truths are simple—
and so are the greatest men.
Chinese Proverb

Too lazy to be ambitious,
I let the world take care of itself.
Ten days worth of rice in my bag;
a bundle of twigs by the fireplace.
Why chatter about delusion and enlightenment?
Learning to listen to the night rain on my roof,
I sit comfortably, with both legs stretched out.
Ryokan

❦

About the Author

Douglas Bloch is an author, lecturer, and seminar leader who writes on the subjects of psychology, healing, and spirituality. In addition to *I Am With You Always*, he is also the author of the inspirational books *Words That Heal: Affirmations and Meditations for Daily Living* and *Listening To Your Inner Voice*.

Mr. Bloch offers lectures and workshops on various aspects of personal development. You may contact him at 4226 NE 23rd Avenue, Portland, OR 97211 (503–284–2848).